Wonderful Wedding

Handmade Napkins

Wrapping Ideas
Cross Knot, One-Touch Ribbon

Handmade Luncheon Mat and Napkins
Wrapping Ideas
Straight Knot, One-Touch Ribbon

KENBERG
P. J. VALCKENBERG
ÜRZIG — MOSEL
1981

Handmade Pot Holder, Pan Holder (Directions on page 8)

Wrapping Ideas
Simple Wrapping, Straight Knot, Pompon Bow

Handmade Pillow Case, Cushion, Bedspread Cover (Directions on page 20)

Wrapping Ideas
Simple Wrapping, Diagonal Wrapping, Straight Knot, Wavy Ribbon, Pompon Bow

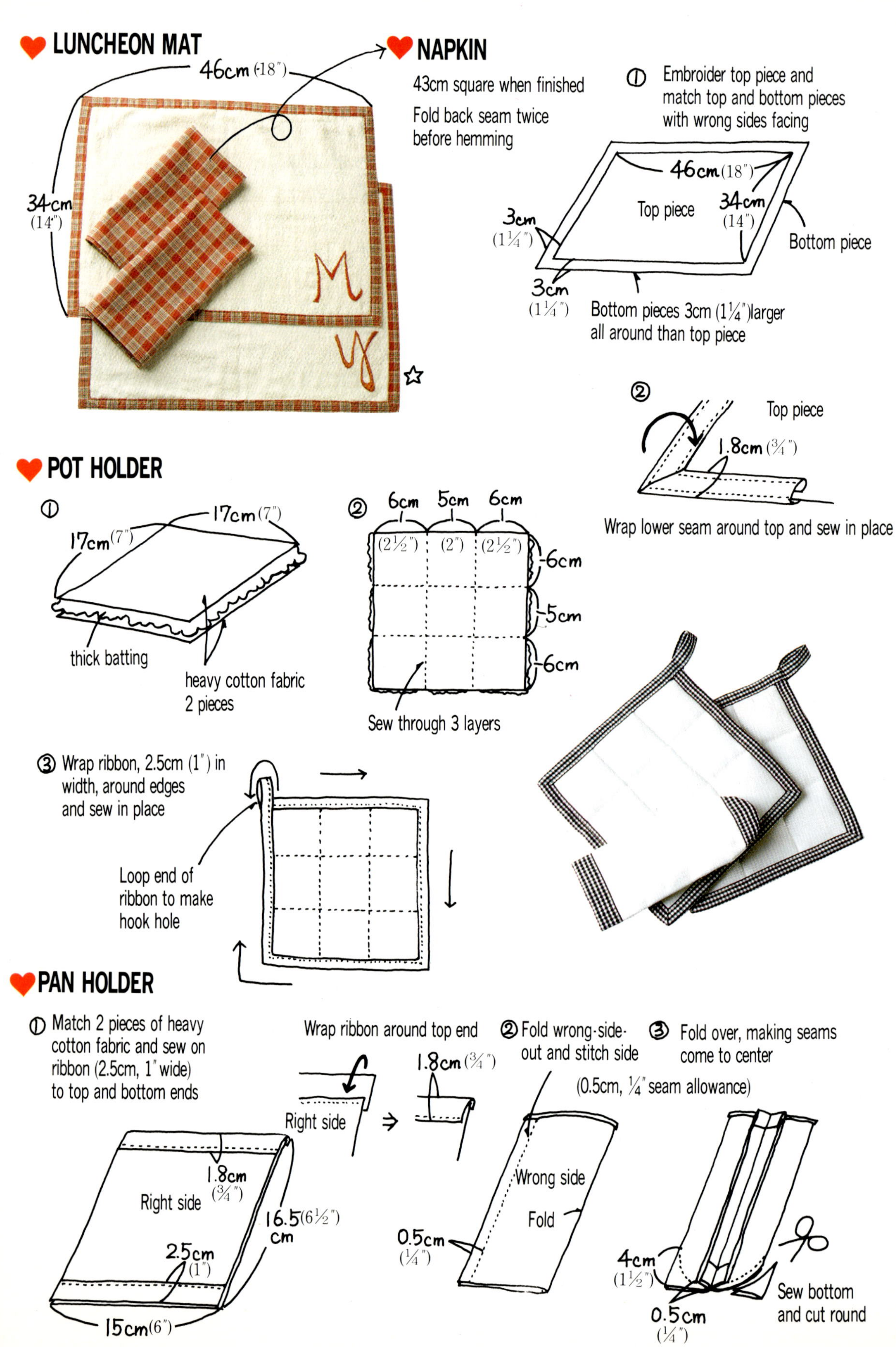

♥ LUNCHEON MAT
46cm (18")
34cm (14")

♥ NAPKIN
43cm square when finished
Fold back seam twice before hemming

① Embroider top piece and match top and bottom pieces with wrong sides facing
46cm (18")
Top piece
34cm (14")
Bottom piece
3cm (1¼")
3cm (1¼")
Bottom pieces 3cm (1¼")larger all around than top piece

② Top piece
1.8cm (¾")
Wrap lower seam around top and sew in place

♥ POT HOLDER
① 17cm (7")
17cm (7")
thick batting
heavy cotton fabric 2 pieces

② 6cm 5cm 6cm
(2½") (2") (2½")
6cm
5cm
6cm
Sew through 3 layers

③ Wrap ribbon, 2.5cm (1") in width, around edges and sew in place
Loop end of ribbon to make hook hole

♥ PAN HOLDER
① Match 2 pieces of heavy cotton fabric and sew on ribbon (2.5cm, 1" wide) to top and bottom ends
Right side
1.8cm (¾")
16.5 (6½") cm
2.5cm (1")
15cm (6")

Wrap ribbon around top end
1.8cm (¾")
Right side

② Fold wrong-side-out and stitch side
(0.5cm, ¼" seam allowance)
Wrong side
Fold
0.5cm (¼")

③ Fold over, making seams come to center
4cm (1½")
0.5cm (¼")
Sew bottom and cut round

Valentine's Day

Wraping Ideas
Straight Knot, Curled Ribbon, One-Touch Ribbon, Wavy Ribbon, Bottle Wrapping

Wrapping Ideas
Simple Wrapping, Diagonal Wrapping, Cylindrical Wrapping,
Candy Wrapping, Bottle Wrapping, Straight Knot, Wavy Ribbon,
Bow Tie Knot, One-Touch Ribbon, Curled Ribbon

Handmade Easy Bags
(Directions on page 16)
Wrapping Ideas
Square Wrapping, Straight Knot,
Bow Tie Knot, Curled Ribbon

Wrapping Ideas
Simple Wrapping, Straight Knot, Diagonal Knot, Cross Knot

EASY BAGS
Checkered type
31cm (12")
46 cm (18")
Fold in loop
Measure includes seam allowance
②
3cm
①
Leave 8cm (3") open
Sew string hole in order of ①② in diagram
Zigzag machine-stitch
Cotton tape, 2cm (¾") in width
Cover edges with felt and fold in when closing
Wrap identical fabric to make matching towel
Cork type
Leather string
13cm (5")
18 cm (7")
Fold in loop
Measure includes seam allowance
(¾")
2cm
Leave 5cm (2") open
Seam allowance not necessary for cork fabric
Bottom edges
2cm (¾")
Hemp type
24 cm (9½")
36 cm (14")
Fold in loop
Measure includes seam allowance
2cm (¾")
Leave 5cm (2") open
Zigzag machine-stitch
Stamp patterns onto cork fabric to make emblems
M
I

A New Start

Wrapping Ideas
Simple Wrapping, Straight Knot, Bow Tie Knot, Wavy Ribbon

For Men

Wrapping Ideas
Diagonal Wrapping, Simple Wrapping, Straight Knot, Cross Knot

For Ladies

Wrapping Ideas
Candy Wrapping, Straight Knot, Bow Tie Knot, Wavy Ribbon

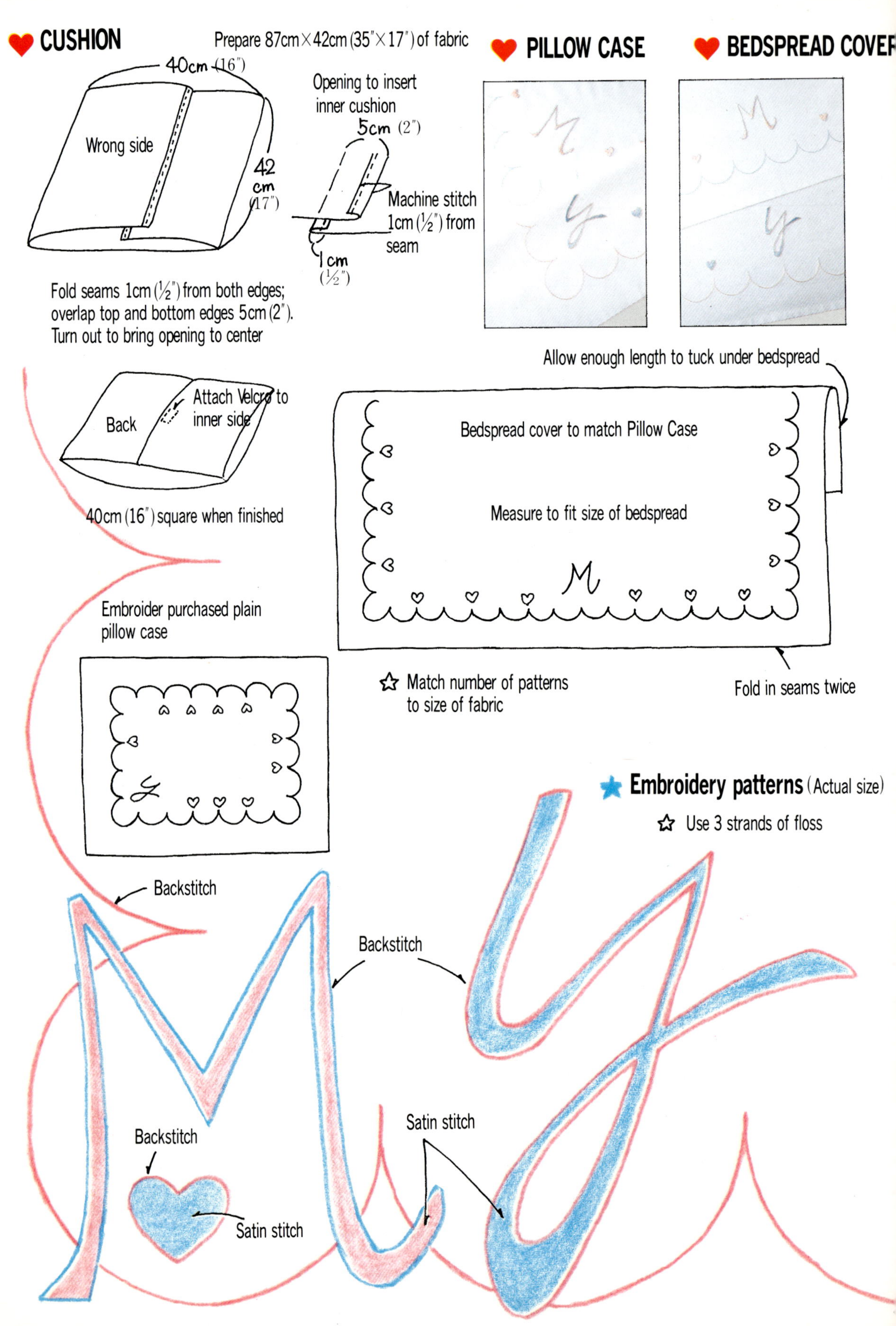

♥ CUSHION

Prepare 87cm×42cm (35″×17″) of fabric

Fold seams 1cm (½″) from both edges; overlap top and bottom edges 5cm (2″). Turn out to bring opening to center

40cm (16″) square when finished

Embroider purchased plain pillow case

♥ PILLOW CASE

♥ BEDSPREAD COVER

Allow enough length to tuck under bedspread

Fold in seams twice

☆ Match number of patterns to size of fabric

★ Embroidery patterns (Actual size)

☆ Use 3 strands of floss

Mother's Day, Father's Day

Handmade Bag

Wrapping Ideas
Simple Wrapping, Double Straight Knot, Diagonal Knot, Straight Knot, Pompon Ribbon

Thanks Mom!

Handmade Apron, Dish Towel, Bags(Directions on page 26)

Wrapping Ideas
Candy Wrapping, Double Straight Knot, Bow Tie Knot, Pompon Ribbon

Thanks Dad!

Wrapping Ideas
Simple Wrapping, Bottle Wrapping,
Cylindrical Wrapping, Straight Knot,
Diagonal Knot, Cross Knot,
Curled Ribbon, Wavy Ribbon

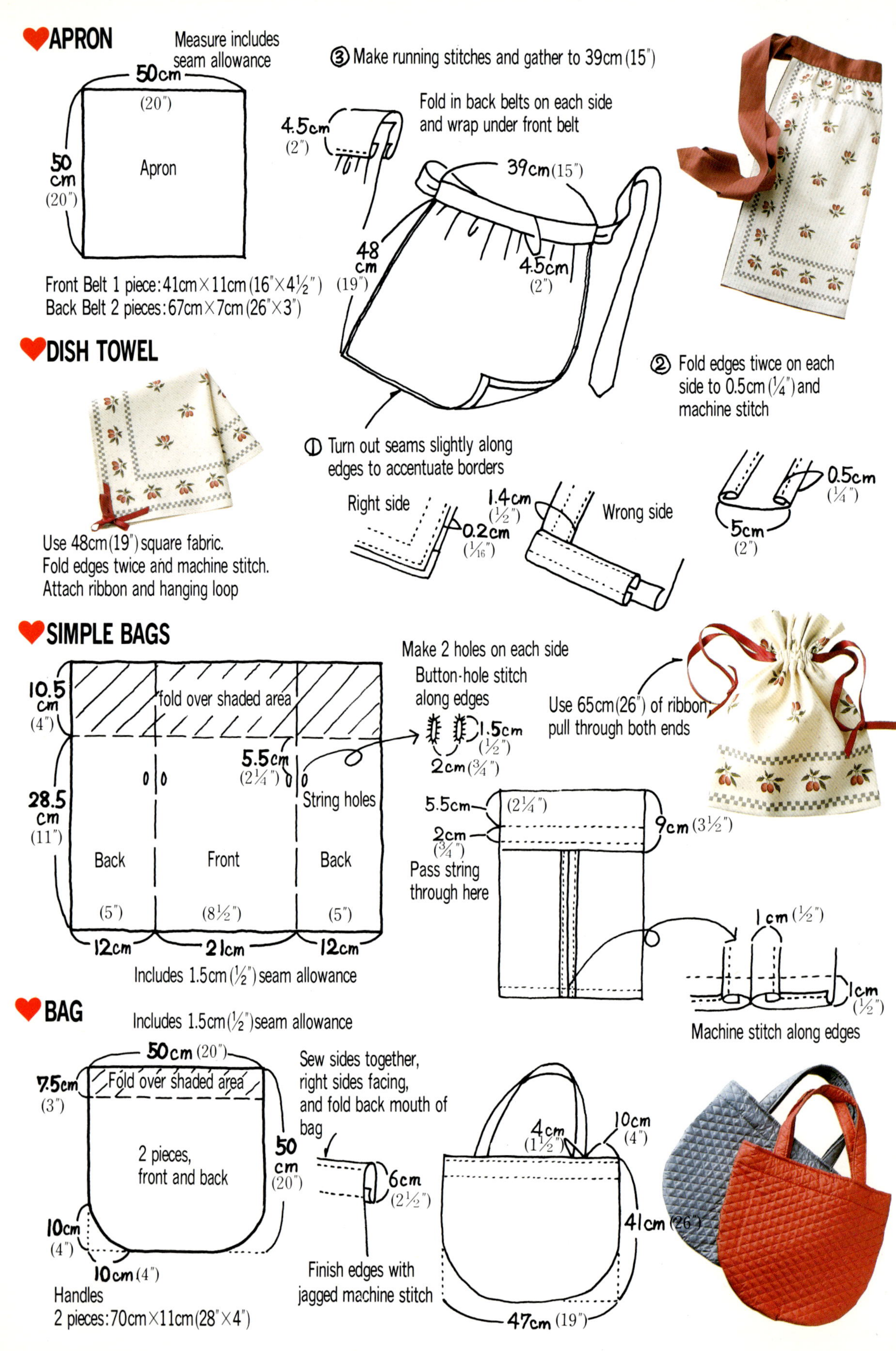

♥APRON

Measure includes seam allowance

50cm (20")

50 cm (20")

Apron

Front Belt 1 piece: 41cm×11cm (16"×4½")
Back Belt 2 pieces: 67cm×7cm (26"×3")

③ Make running stitches and gather to 39cm (15")

Fold in back belts on each side and wrap under front belt

4.5cm (2")

39cm (15")

48 cm (19")

4.5cm (2")

♥DISH TOWEL

Use 48cm (19") square fabric.
Fold edges twice and machine stitch.
Attach ribbon and hanging loop

① Turn out seams slightly along edges to accentuate borders

Right side

1.4cm (½")

0.2cm (1/16")

Wrong side

② Fold edges tiwce on each side to 0.5cm (¼") and machine stitch

0.5cm (¼")

5cm (2")

♥SIMPLE BAGS

10.5 cm (4")

fold over shaded area

5.5cm (2¼")

0 0

String holes

28.5 cm (11")

0 0

0 0

Back

Front

Back

(5")

(8½")

(5")

12cm

21cm

12cm

Includes 1.5cm (½") seam allowance

Make 2 holes on each side
Button-hole stitch along edges

1.5cm (½")

2cm (¾")

Use 65cm (26") of ribbon;
pull through both ends

5.5cm (2¼")

2cm (¾")

9cm (3½")

Pass string through here

1cm (½")

1cm (½")

Machine stitch along edges

♥BAG

Includes 1.5cm (½") seam allowance

50cm (20")

7.5cm (3")

Fold over shaded area

2 pieces, front and back

50 cm (20")

10cm (4")

10cm (4")

Handles
2 pieces: 70cm×11cm (28"×4")

Sew sides together, right sides facing, and fold back mouth of bag

6cm (2½")

Finish edges with jagged machine stitch

4cm (1½")

10cm (4")

41cm (26")

47cm (19")

For the New Baby

Handmade Stuffed Animals (Directions on page 32)

Wrapping Ideas
Straight Knot, Pompon Ribbon

Handmade Bib, Underclothes
Wrapping Ideas
Cross Knot, Pompon Ribbon

Wrapping Ideas
Pompon Ribbon

Baby born
to moi
Baby Born

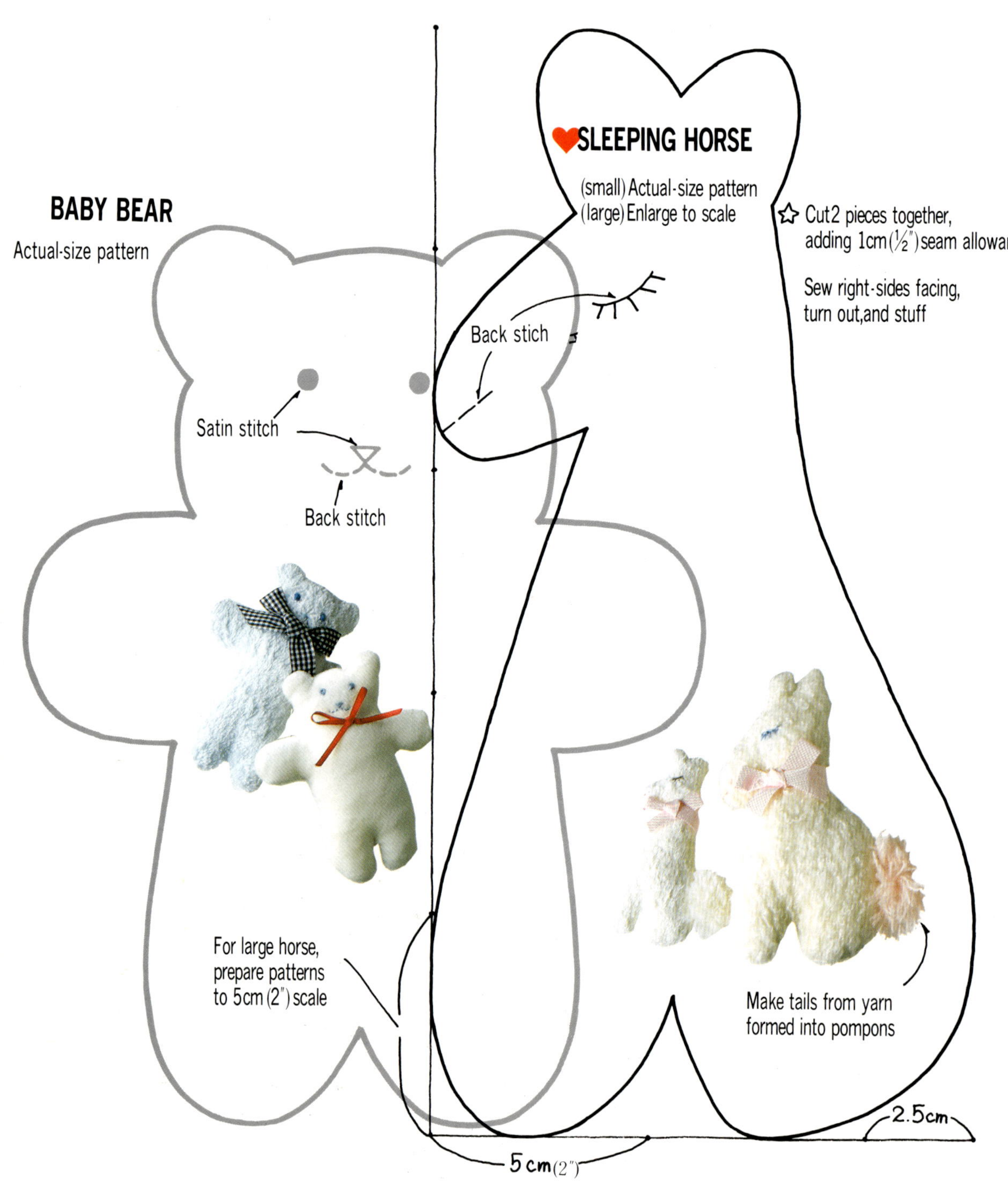

BABY BEAR
Actual-size pattern

Satin stitch
Back stitch

SLEEPING HORSE
(small) Actual-size pattern
(large) Enlarge to scale
Cut 2 pieces together,
adding 1cm (½") seam allowance

Sew right-sides facing,
turn out, and stuff

Back stich

For large horse,
prepare patterns
to 5cm (2") scale

Make tails from yarn
formed into pompons

2.5cm

5 cm (2")

Happy Birthday!

Wrapping Ideas
Square Wrapping, Simple Wrapping, Straight Knot,
Double Straight Knot, Curled Ribbon, One-Touch Ribbon

Wrapping Ideas
Cylindrical Wrapping, Straight Knot, Wavy Ribbon

Wrapping Ideas
Simple Wrapping, Square Wrapping, Straight Knot, Double Straight Knot,
Curled Ribbon, One–Touch Ribbon

LATE NEWS
ROD STEWART
Happy Birthday to yoji

Merry Christmas!

Wrapping Ideas
Diagonal Wrapping, Square Wrapping, Simple Wrapping, Straight Knot,
Cross Knot, Diagonal Knot, Pompon Ribbon, Wavy Ribbon

Wrapping Ideas
Simple Wrapping, Square Wrapping, Straight Knot, Double Straight Knot,
Cross Knot, Curled Ribbon, One-Touch Ribbon

"bearly there"
COMPANY
Fountain Valley, Ca. 92708
cuddly brown

Homemade Goodies

Wrapping Ideas
Square Wrapping, Straight Knot, Cross Knot,
Curled Ribbon, One-Touch Ribbon

42

HAND MADE

Gift Cards

JUST FOR YOU
greeting
Season's greeting
HaPPY Birthday
to Papa
Hello
Summer!
HELLO
GREETINGS
bonjour

JUST FOR YOU
11月9日
PM, 7時より
Th. party
おとうさん
ありがとう

Hints on
Wrapping and Tying

① Bottle Wrapping

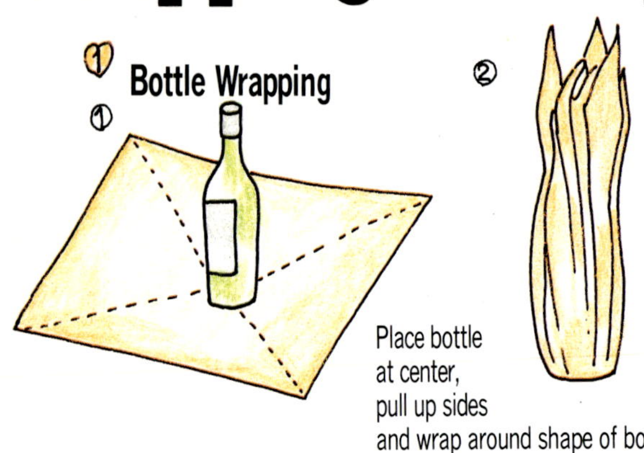

Place bottle
at center,
pull up sides
and wrap around shape of bottle

② Candy Wrapping

Wrap around object

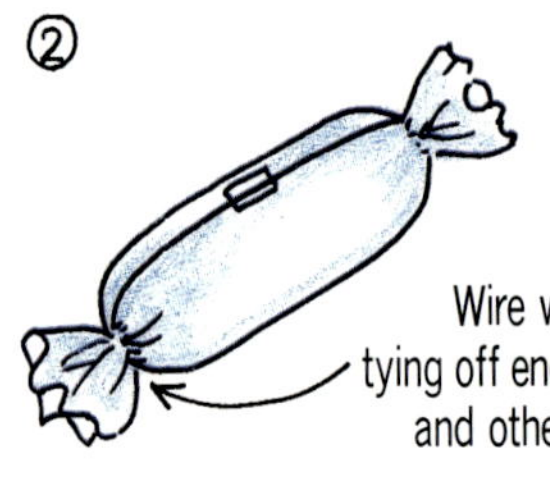

Wire works well when
tying off ends of cellophane
and other soft materials

③ Cylindrical Wrapping

Place object at right
angle to diagonal line

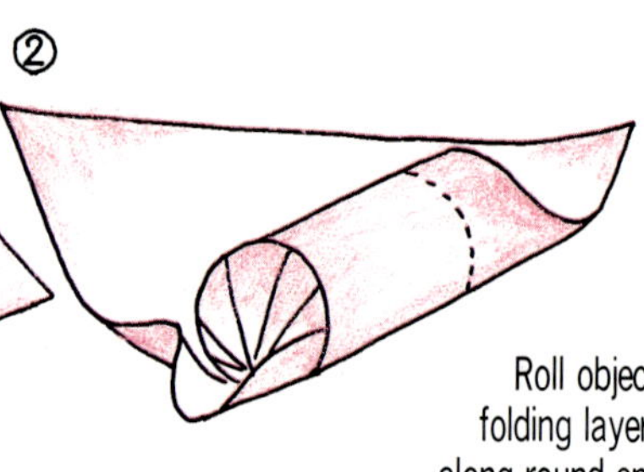

Roll object,
folding layers
along round end

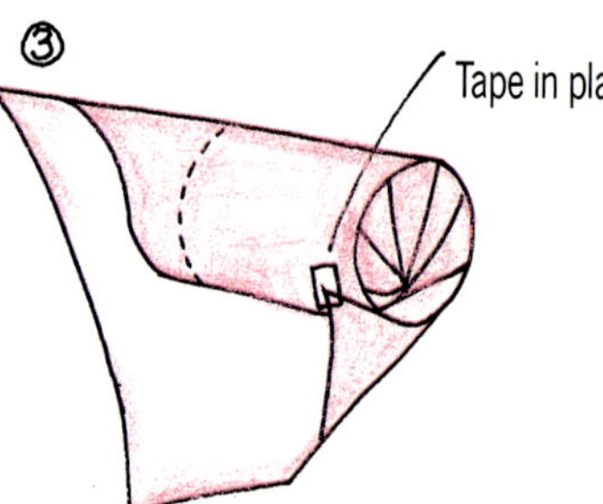

When object has been completely
covered, fold in any excess material

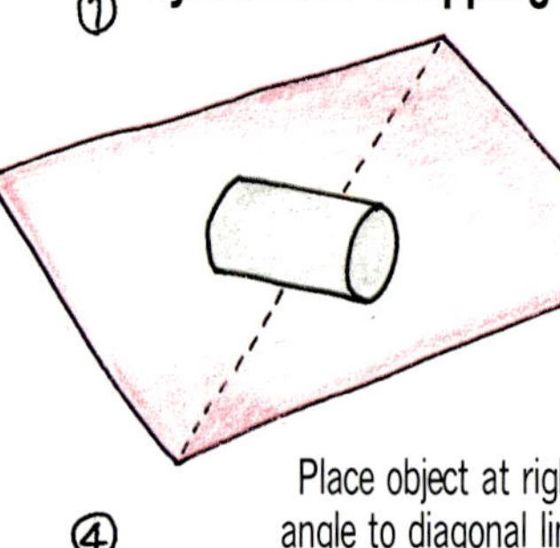

Fold layers along other end in same manner

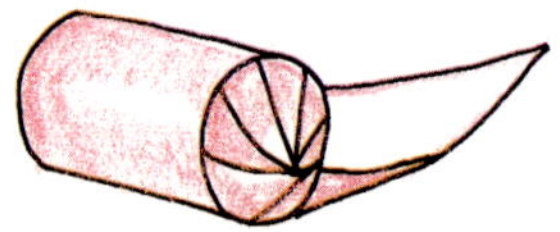
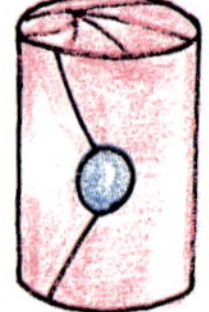

When working with oil paper,
rub paper file over surface
where tape will be used

Instead of tape, try using
stickers to brighten up your gift

④ Circular Wrapping

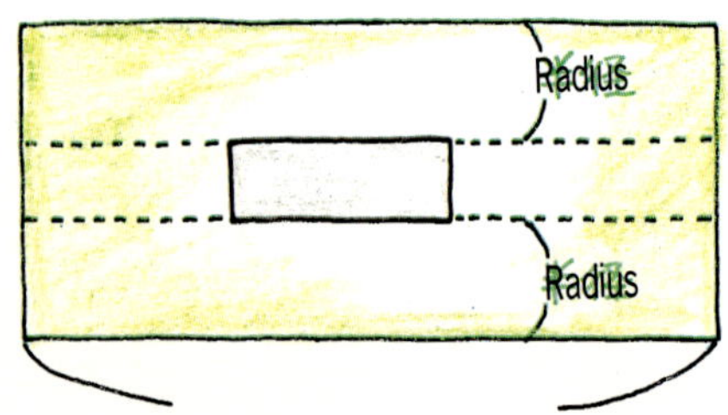

Circumference and overlapping area

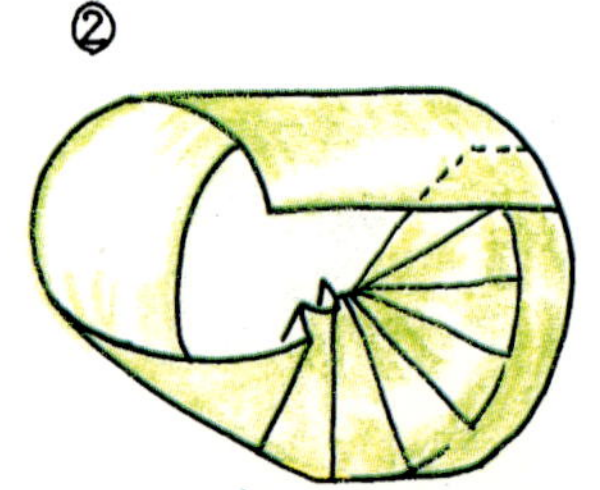

Fold in ends, making even layers

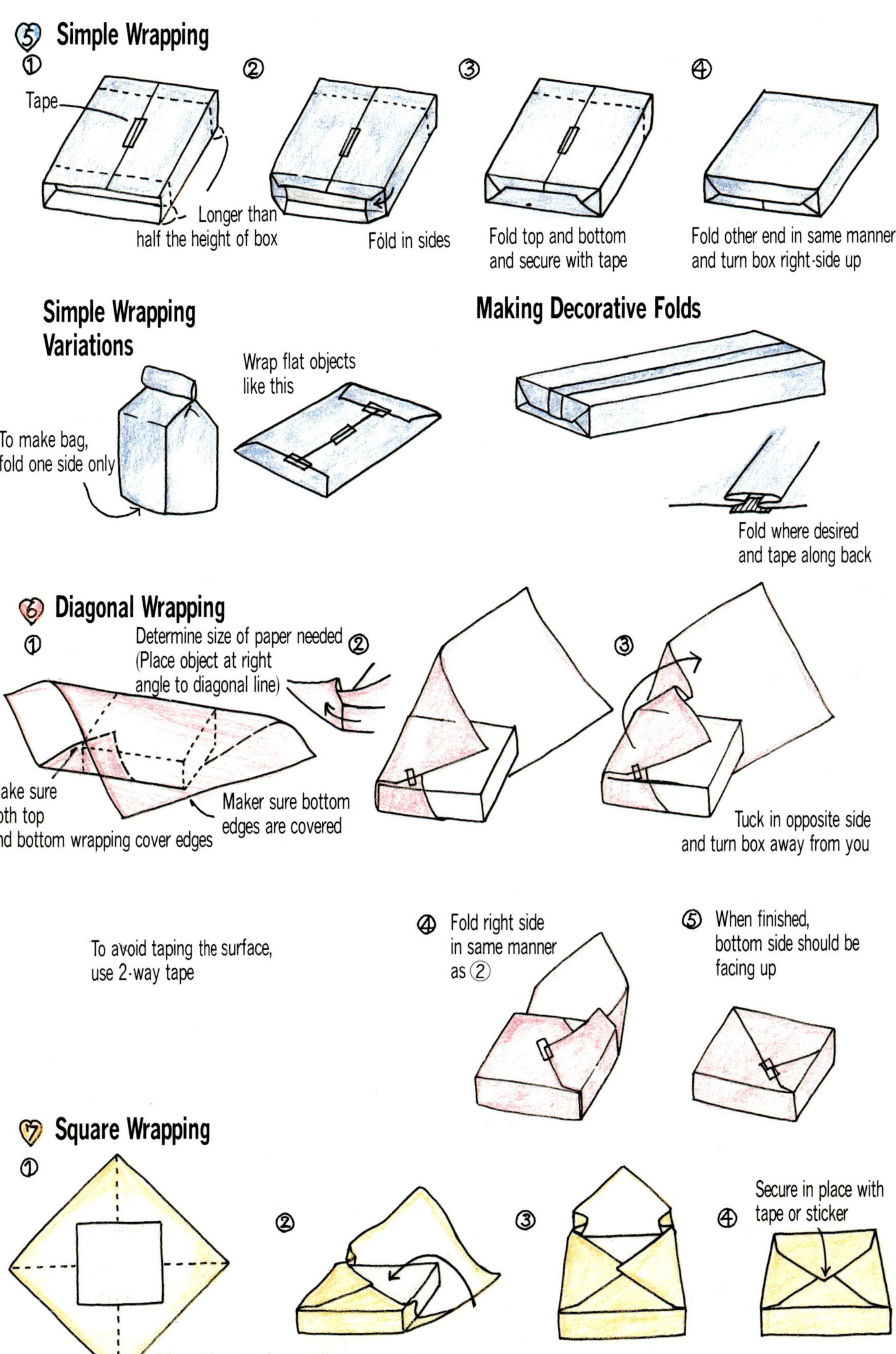

⑤ Simple Wrapping
①
Tape
Longer than half the height of box
②
Fold in sides
③
Fold top and bottom and secure with tape
④
Fold other end in same manner and turn box right-side up
Simple Wrapping Variations
To make bag, fold one side only
Wrap flat objects like this
Making Decorative Folds
Fold where desired and tape along back
⑥ Diagonal Wrapping
①
Determine size of paper needed (Place object at right angle to diagonal line)
Make sure both top and bottom wrapping cover edges
Maker sure bottom edges are covered
②
③
Tuck in opposite side and turn box away from you
To avoid taping the surface, use 2-way tape
④ Fold right side in same manner as ②
⑤ When finished, bottom side should be facing up
⑦ Square Wrapping
①
②
③
④ Secure in place with tape or sticker
Place object on diagonal lines

Tying Ribbons

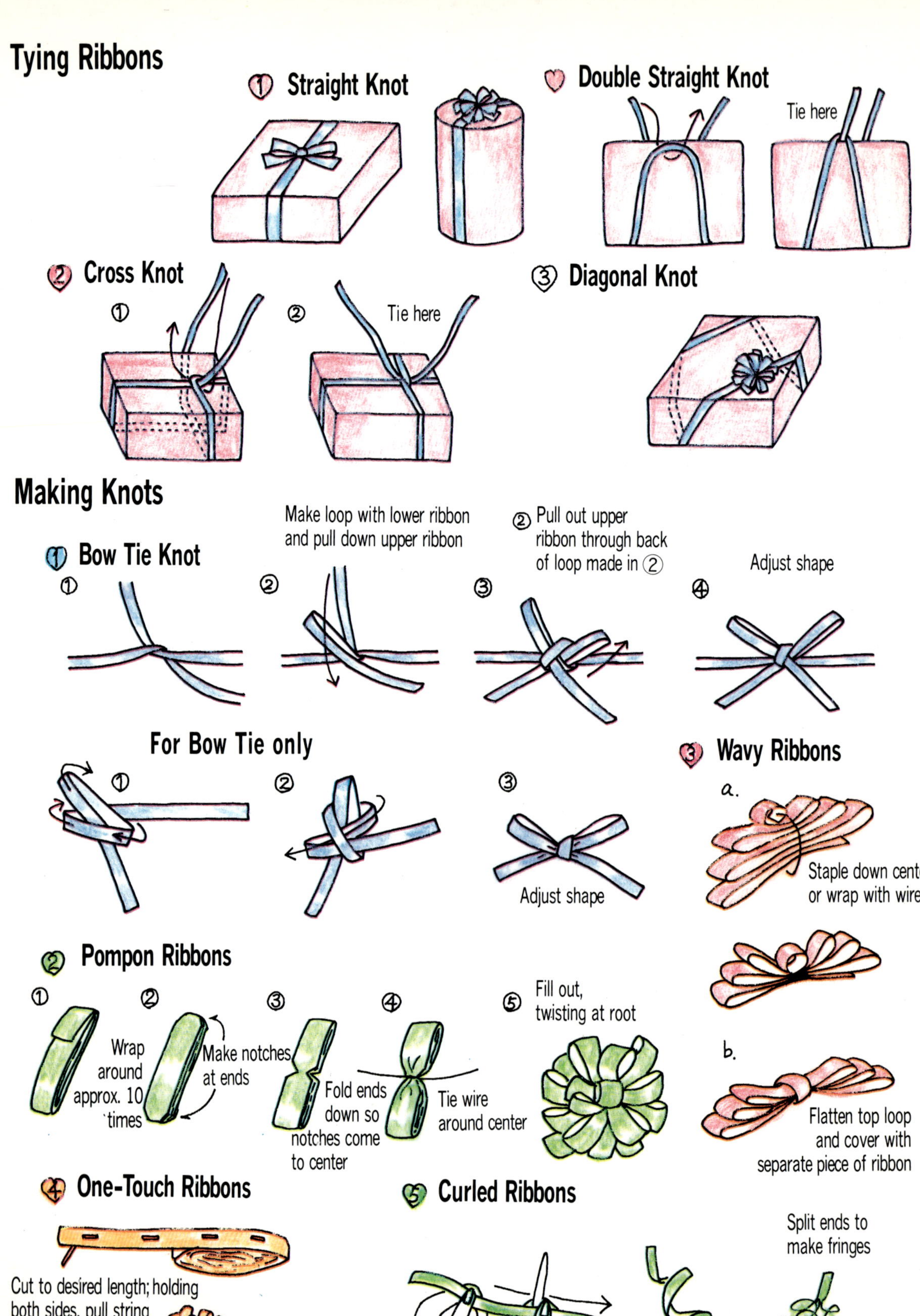